CLEVER CARBS

Written by
John Wood

Published in 2022 by Enslow Publishing, LLC
29 East 21st Street, New York, NY 10010

Copyright © 2021 Booklife Publishing
This edition is published by arrangement with Booklife Publishing

All rights reserved.

No part of this book may be reproduced by any means without the written permission of the publisher.

Cataloging-in-Publication Data

Names: Wood, John, 1990-.
Title: Clever carbs / John Wood.
Description: New York : Enslow Publishing, 2022. | Series: Brain food | Includes glossary and index.
Identifiers: ISBN 9781978523760 (pbk.) | ISBN 9781978523784 (library bound) | ISBN 9781978523777 (6 pack) | ISBN 9781978523791 (ebook)
Subjects: LCSH: Carbohydrates in human nutrition--Juvenile literature. | Nutrition--Juvenile literature.
Classification: LCC QP701.W66 2022 | DDC 613.2--dc23

Designer: Jasmine Pointer
Editor: William Anthony

Printed in the United States of America

CPSIA compliance information: Batch #CSENS22. For further information contact Enslow Publishing, New York, New York at 1-800-398-2504

PHOTO CREDITS

All images are courtesy of Shutterstock.com, unless otherwise specified. With thanks to Getty Images, Thinkstock Photo and iStockphoto.

Scientist character throughout — Designbypex. Cover — Nattika, Maks Narodenko, tetxu, GOLFX. 4–5 — denizya. 6–7 — Africa Studio, Carlos Horta, Ann in the uk. 8–9 — Gamzova Olga, baibaz, Hanna_photo, mama_mia. 10–11 — Shyamalamuralinath. 12–13 — rodrigobark, kornnphoto. 14–15 — Joe Gough, J.Dream. 16–17 — Liliya Kandrashevich, Roquillo Tebar. 18–19 — Amawasri Pakdara, Roquillo Tebar. 20–21 — Supitcha McAdam, bigacis, uladzimir zgurski, wavebreakmedia. 22–23 — TrotzOlga, DONOT6_STUDIO, Africa Studio, BW Folsom, ifong.

CONTENTS

Page 4   A Slice of Science
Page 6   Portions
Page 8   What Are Carbs?
Page 10 Let's Experiment!
Page 12 Speed Boost
Page 14 Can I Have Some More?
Page 16 Lunch for Learning
Page 18 Burning Fat
Page 20 Food Swaps
Page 23 The Most Important Thing
Page 24 Glossary and Index

Words that look like this can be found in the glossary on page 24.

A SLICE OF SCIENCE

Is someone telling you that you're eating too much? Does your mom say to eat more fruit? You might be wondering: why does it matter what I eat?

Hello! I'm a small scientist. I'm here to teach you about food. Food is very important!

You might have heard the words "healthy diet." A diet is the kinds of food you usually eat. To have a healthy diet, you need to make sure you eat the right amount of different foods.

A healthy diet is often called a <u>balanced</u> diet because you eat lots of different types of food.

PORTIONS

A portion, or serving, of food is the amount you eat in one sitting. It can be <u>measured</u> in ounces.

You use a food scale like this to weigh food in ounces.

A portion of food might be one banana.

The right portion size is different for every food. You should have about five servings of fruits and vegetables a day. A serving of fruit is roughly the amount you can fit in the palm of your hand.

WHAT ARE CARBS?

Carbohydrates, or carbs, are one of the main kinds of <u>nutrients</u> found in food. Their main job is to give you <u>energy</u>.

Let's have a look at some foods that have lots of carbs in them.

Cereal

Bread

Sweet potatoes

Bananas

9

LET'S EXPERIMENT!

"We will need this mood bar. It will tell us about someone's body. It shows four things — how much energy they have, how hungry they are, how much their head hurts, and how smelly their breath is!"

ENERGY

HUNGER

HEADACHES

BREATH SMELLINESS

SPEED BOOST

Let's give him some rice! Rice is a <u>starchy</u> carb. We should eat starchy carbs every day because they are a great way to get energy.

Starchy foods also have lots of nutrients.

CAN I HAVE SOME MORE?

She didn't eat enough carbohydrates with her meal! Let's give her some potatoes. Many carbs also have other things in them too, such as <u>fiber</u>.

Potato skins have lots of healthy things in them, so it is a good idea to keep them on!

LUNCH FOR LEARNING

How about pasta? Like other carbs, pasta helps your body make <u>blood sugar</u>. Blood sugar gives you energy, and without it you would feel tired and grumpy. Low blood sugar can also give you a headache.

<u>Whole grain</u> pasta is a good choice! Turn to page 20 to learn more about whole grains.

BURNING FAT

There are carbs in all sorts of beans, such as black beans, baked beans, and kidney beans.

Let's give this kid beans! When you stop getting energy from carbs, your body burns fat instead. But burning fat can make your breath stink!

FOOD SWAPS

Whole grain carbs are a great choice. Here are some examples of whole grain carbs.

Whole wheat bread

Brown rice

Whole wheat pasta

This girl is testing her blood sugar levels.

Diabetes is a disease that causes problems with blood sugar. Unlike carbs such as white rice or white bread, whole grain carbs change blood sugar levels more slowly. This is better for people who have diabetes.

THE MOST IMPORTANT THING

Carbohydrates are a great source of energy for your body! However, don't forget that it's important to eat lots of different types of food. That is what makes a diet healthy and balanced!

Carbs
Fruits and vegetables
Protein
Fats and sugars
Dairy

GLOSSARY

balanced	made up of the right or equal amounts
blood sugar	a type of sugar called glucose that is moved around the body in your blood
energy	the ability to do something
fiber	a part of some foods that takes longer for the human body to break down
measured	to have found out the exact amount of something using units or systems, such as ounces for weight or feet for distance
nutrients	things that plants and animals need to grow and stay healthy
starchy	full of lots of starch, which is a tasteless, white part of food from plants
whole grain	containing the whole of the grain seed

INDEX

beans 18
bread 20–21
breath 10, 17–18
cereal 8
dairy 22–23
diabetes 21
diets 5, 14, 23
energy 8, 10–12, 16, 18
fat 18, 23
fruit 4, 7, 9, 22–23
headaches 10, 15–16
hunger 10, 13
pasta 16, 20
portions 6–7
potatoes 9, 14
rice 12, 20–21